A Mere Christian
Ron Smith, MD

~⊛ Snowy House ⊛~

A Mere Christian

Ron Smith, MD

Snowy House
First print edition, version 1.0.1, 20,600 words.
Cover design by Ron Smith, MD
Edited by Stacy Smith
Copyright ©2014 Ron Smith, MD
All rights reserved.
ISBN: 0-9858239-2-5
ISBN-13: 978-0-9858239-2-4

Note: All quotations from the Holy Bible are from the King James Version unless otherwise noted.

To

Andréa
a virtuous daughter

&

Laura Michelle
now complete in Christ

About The Author

EARLY IN 2012 at the age of twenty-four, my youngest daughter Laura Michelle passed away. She was severely disabled from birth, and her ongoing physical problems became increasingly intense right up to her sudden passing.

Stacy and I had been married almost thirty-five years then, and were both solid Christians since early childhood. Like a red hot forge, Laura's illness burned away thoughts and ideas which were wrong-headed and even destructive. Everything we believed was reweighed and remeasured. The accumulated dross of daily living was discarded as we became stronger and deeper in our faith.

For several years even prior to her passing, I had been listening to *Mere Christianity* every day on my half-hour commute to and from work. Later I found Knox Chamblin's wonderful iTunes U course on C. S. Lewis and began listening to it as well.

Late in 2012 our small congregation at Senoia United Methodist Church began a turbulent change in pastors. Some of us faired poorly through it and it made me see the need for our small body of believers to understand what Lewis and Chamblin had been teaching me. Early in 2013, I started teaching *Mere Christianity* in our adult Sunday School class. I think it was then that I realized why I had been schooled by these wonderful men whose words of truth echo beyond their passing.

By no means do I claim to be anything at all other than that I'm a true believer in Jesus Christ. What has come out of all those hours of study and teaching I have now put down for all to benefit. That is my only goal.

Ron Smith, MD
A Mere Christian
March 26, 2014

Our Spiritual Anatomy

Body
(Flesh)

Soul
(Heart)

Spirit
(Mind)

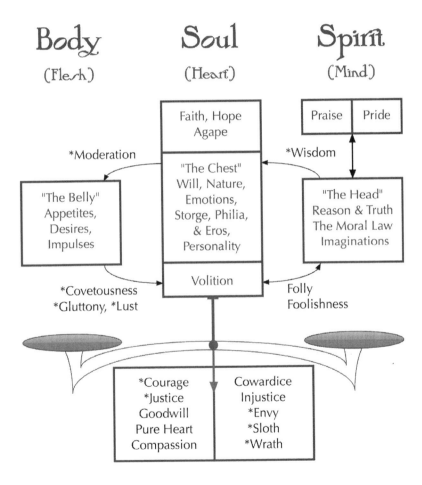

Faith, Hope
Agape

Praise | Pride

*Moderation

*Wisdom

"The Chest"
Will, Nature,
Emotions,
Storge, Philia,
& Eros,
Personality

"The Belly"
Appetites,
Desires,
Impulses

"The Head"
Reason & Truth
The Moral Law
Imaginations

Volition

*Covetousness
*Gluttony, *Lust

Folly
Foolishness

*Courage
*Justice
Goodwill
Pure Heart
Compassion

Cowardice
Injustice
*Envy
*Sloth
*Wrath

Table of Contents

Preface

Quid ubique creditur ab omnibus semper[1]

A Mere Christian, is extremely indebted to C. S. Lewis and *Mere Christianity*. His incomparable work originated as a series of three broadcast radio talks in Great Britain during World War II. I owe many thanks also to the late Knox Chamblin, Ph.D., professor at Reformed Theological Seminary. His iTunes U course on C. S. Lewis taught me a great deal. These admirable men stood pointing me to our Lord and Savior Jesus Christ, who alone is worthy of praise.

At nine, Jack's mother Flora was diagnosed with cancer. Before she died later that same year, she presented Jack and his brother Warren each with a Bible. God was certainly drawing him at a young age, and perhaps he was even then a true believer in Christ.

Jack's father, Albert, really never got over Flora. Unable to provide her same emotional support and security, he soon sent both boys off to boarding schools. While boarding at Cherbourg House, Lewis declared himself an atheist.

While Warnie was at Malvern College, Lewis also lived in Malvern studying under William T. Kirkpatrick, a tutor whose nickname was the Great Knock. He was a rigorously aggressive, logical thinker. He was also an atheist. Kirkpatrick played no small part in Jack's successful entrance to Oxford university. He went on to become a tutor and then a fellow there. It was also at Oxford that he surrendered to God's draw.

In 1929, Jack could no longer deny God's existence. The intellect that had once wrested God from him, now forced him to reject atheism. It was in his rooms in Oxford, that he bowed his knees and prayed to God. He stated that he was the most reluctant convert in all of England.

On September 22, 1931, he was sitting in the sidecar of Warnie's motorcycle on the way to Whipsnade Zoo. When they left, he didn't believe that Christ was God, and when he arrived he did.

What happened in Jack's life to effect such a dramatic change? *What was he thinking* that convinced him of Christ and allowed, nay caused, him to become a different man? These questions have become pervasive in my own life.

Walter Hooper, his personal secretary near the end of his life, called him the most thoroughly converted man he ever knew. Pain and trials are a fact of our lives, and Lewis had his share. They were no doubt strong antidotes to pride. His humility stirs me.

"I am a very ordinary layman of the Church of England, not especially 'high,' nor especially 'low,' nor especially anything else." –C. S. Lewis[2]

My purpose in writing *A Mere Christian* is of course to share what I've gleaned from Lewis, Chamblin, and others. The closer we get to the ever-certain return of Christ for his Church, the more God makes us to understand what has previously been mystery. Our view of that return is closer than was Jack's and more of God's mystery is revealed.

Christians are not buckets to be filled, but fires to be kindled. What Christians believe and do is more important than what happens to us. Above all, *A Mere Christian* stands with fellow believers, shouting to the world just how great is our God!

Ron Smith, MD
December 30, 2013

CHAPTER ONE

At The Same Time

A man put it to me by saying 'I can believe in God all right, but what I cannot swallow is the idea of Him attending to several hundred million human beings who are all addressing Him at the same moment.' -C. S. Lewis[3]

I REMEMBER PONDERING this very same sticky problem as a small boy. Though I wondered about all the other children praying at the same time, it really never occurred to me to doubt God's ability to fully attend to each and every prayer. Surely God must have it all worked out somehow. Being a little boy, I accepted his abilities at face value.

But how can even God sort out so many voices at once?

I think the question really is not only a very good one. It is a very important one. The answer goes far beyond what I expected or imagined. When I understood the answer, it was like putting on magic glasses that opened up a clearer view of God's Word!

Surprisingly, the answer starts with knowing how science works.

Science

I was just four when I started talking about being a doctor. My road to medicine went through Chemistry, deep within the territory of pure science. Being a committed Christian *and* a scientist meant that I had to understand the bounds of science. Modern culture prompts us to think that anything that science says must really be the truth, even when it is not.

science |ˈsīəns| *n., the intellectual and practical activity encompassing the systematic study of the structure and behavior of the physical and natural world through observation and experiment: the world of science and technology.*[4]

Above is the definition from my computer's dictionary. Notice how this describes *scientific method*, which is the core of all true science. A scientist considers and then proposes how something in nature might work. He devises experimental methods to provide accurate observations to see if his hypothesis is true. Accurate analysis of the results and the methods will yield either a conclusion about the hypothesis or produce indeterminate results.

A simple illustration demonstrates scientific method. A scientist puts a sample of pure metal in a crucible with a thermometer and heats it. He observes and records the melting point. Good science requires that this experiment be repeated for accuracy since things like impurities in the metal or variations in the heat source will alter the observed melting point.

Verification by repeat experimentation is an essential part of science. Science must let the experiment run and the unbiased results fall where they may. It must seek to identify points of failure, so that the experiment can be improved to get the most reliable and highest quality results. Accuracy in observation is the highest goal in pure science.

All knowledge is not science, however. Unlike chemistry, history is not science at all. Events in time cannot be rerun like scientific experiments.

Certain fields such as archeology and paleontology have unfortunate pitfalls. Observations of fossils and geology can give you scientific data about those animals remains, but they cannot tell you exactly how they lived.

Tyrannosaurus Rex was originally thought to be an aggressive lion-like predator. It was later demoted to a vulture-like scavenger almost strictly on the basis of the shorter forearms which seemed useless in hunting. We will probably never know this as a fact because it is not subject to pure scientific method. Without observing a live T. Rex, we really don't know why those forelegs were so small. Such conclusions stray into personal opinion and subjective bias.

So-called authoritative conclusions based on speculation are clearly outside the bounds of science. Opinions may be a useful starting point from which to frame a sound scientific experiment, but they are illegitimate if presented alone as scientific truth.

Scientific 'opinion' is quite often self-serving. Many scientists are funded by research grants and they only get paid if they produce results. More spectacular results may bring more grant money. Financial reward often outweighs truthful results.

Such was the case of one Andrew Wakefield who startled the world with his claim that the MMR vaccine caused autism. It took some fourteen years to be disproven and repudiated in the *Lancet*, the well-known British medical journal where it was originally published. His intentionally jiggered results harmed children who contracted measles as a result of not being vaccinated.

More importantly though science cannot tell you why and how things came to be in the first place. Trying to determine the origin of everything based only on the fossil records, geologic evidence, or astronomical observation is a mess. You always come back to the old question about which came first, the chicken or the egg.

To even consider that *either* the chicken or the egg came first implies a sentient creative force. For many scientists that is simply unacceptable. They will close their ears to any such talk of an infinitely powerful being. At the same time many of them propose searching for advanced alien beings who may have visited our planet from other far-flung worlds. They can't have it both ways.

Even if alien life were found, we would still be faced with the chicken-and-egg question. If God is to be denied, then that question must be deferred.

To that end, scientists have long proposed the idea of a primordial soup as the origin of nature. They conclude that from the right mixture of lightning, heat, and temperature, all life must have sprung forth and evolved from warm, nutrient-rich pools of water. The primordial soup theory is however not amenable to scientific method nor is it verified in fossil records which show no evidence of a continuously slow and smooth variation of change in biologic organisms. Failings in the fossil record must have new theories like interrupted evolutionary development.

Not all scientists support such theories, but few seem to step forward and challenge them for fear of being outed as politically incorrect idiots. It is easy to understand their fear. For them it is not just research grant money at stake, but their very livelihood.

Some Christians and a few scientists believe that evolution was God's chosen method for our creation. Though that is not my opinion, these folks have at least not dishonestly used science as an attempt to exclude God.

There is really only one answer to the chicken-and-egg dilemma. Scientific arrogancy insists that at all costs any creator must be excluded. Unfortunately, the more that scientists discover using valid scientific method, the more they find which cannot be explained without a creator.

In The Beginning

Several years ago, I was able to take two semesters of freshman astronomy. Astronomy combines chemistry, physics, and geology in a way that fascinates me. One day my professor described the ever-expanding universe starting at the beginning as it was thought to have been. At time zero, and from nothing, the cataclysmic expansion of all the matter that is, or ever will be, starts. No one knows why or how it is expanding, or what it is expanding into. This is called the Big Bang theory.

Scientists do think they have some idea about how things might have progressed just beyond time zero. The four distinguishable forces within the expanding matter became apparent probably in this order: gravity, the strong nuclear force, electromagnetic attraction, and the weak nuclear force. At 10^{-43} seconds gravity split off and the temperature of the universe was 10^{32} degrees Kelvin. By 10^{-10} seconds all the other forces had split off and the universe had cooled to 10^{15} degrees Kelvin.

Take a deep breath and consider the sizes of these numbers. When you write 10^{32} degrees Kelvin, that is the number 1 with 32 zeroes following it. It is unimaginably hot. It took matter almost 400,000 years to cool to the point that even the hydrogen atom existed.

When you write 10^{-43} seconds that is a decimal point with forty-two zeroes followed by the number one. This small time interval is staggering. For comparison, the boiling point of water is just 373 degrees Kelvin which is the same as 212° Fahrenheit or 100° Celsius. Cesium atomic clocks are very accurate and vary only by 2 billionths or 2×10^{-9} seconds a day.

So science believes that somehow the universe, i.e., time and space, began out of nothing at a singular point, and was a uniform mixture of the smallest atomic building blocks. Science does not know what contained this point in space where everything began. So how does it come to this conclusion?

From the best observations, there are limits to the light that can be seen to suggest that the universe does not go on forever. It has an outer expanding edge. Many years ago, astronomers began seeing measurements of light from distant stars. They discovered something amazing. Not only is everything expanding, but all stars are moving away from all other points in all directions. The very substance of space it seems is inflating. Even more shocking, they found the rate of expansion is ever increasing and not running down. In other words everything is accelerating away from everything else.

Several centuries ago scientists discovered that there were key observable behaviors of matter. So significant were these behaviors they pronounced these behaviors the Laws of Thermodynamics. The Laws of Thermodynamics are not hard to understand.

The Zero Law of Thermodynamics says that if two systems are in equilibrium with a third system then they are in equilibrium with each other. That is like saying in arithmetic that if one plus two equals three and five minus two equals three, then one plus two also equals five minus two.

What this Law is essentially saying is that all the energy that ever was in the universe is all that there ever will be. Energy is always conserved in the form of matter and within space.

The First Law of Thermodynamics builds on the Zero Law and says that energy flows downhill. That means that energy spreads out. For this reason there can never be a perpetual motion machine. All the energy that you put into the machine will 'flow' out of the machine as it runs down. Heat, i.e., energy, always moves away to colder surroundings.

The Second Law of Thermodynamics builds on the First Law and says that as this energy flows to the surroundings, matter becomes more disordered and distant from other matter. Things continually get more disorganized in other words. The scientific term for this disorganization is entropy.

The Third Law of Thermodynamics builds on the Second Law and says that as the disorder of matter increases the temperature will eventually become zero once matter is completely disorganized. All energy will be evenly spread out over all of space. All movement will cease and the temperature will be absolute zero.

At once, we see there are significant problems reconciling the astronomical findings with these scientifically hallowed laws of nature. How can the universe be accelerating in its expansion if things are supposed to run down? More importantly how do you figure the universe got all that energy to start out of nothing in the first place?

The Laws of Thermodynamics do not exist outside of time and space as we know it. More importantly, something is happening to our universe in this accelerating expansion that these Laws also cannot explain.

Time, A Prisoner

Why the universe burst into existence out of nothing is called the primary or *First Cause* of creation. Science can never tell us the First Cause of the universe. So why does it exist in the first place? Science cannot explain how the accelerating expansion of the universe defies the Laws of Thermodynamics.

Some of the common responses seem to be theories about a previous universe that expanded and contracted like a rubber band. But that doesn't fit either. There appears to be no contraction of the universe in sight and the observed acceleration will end up putting all particles of matter increasingly further from all other particles of matter.

This is the point where science ends and philosophy begins. Philosophical arguments about the beginnings have traditionally been centered on the literal translation of Genesis, as fostered by many. Scientists who are opposed to any philosophical arguments about the beginnings often give even childish explanations which they seek to proffer as science. The truth is that no matter how learned these scientists are, anything they say about the First Cause of the universe is purely personal, non-authoritative philosophical speculation.

It is not science, and *everyone* is a philosopher.

Those that object to a creator of time and space oppose the idea that these entities are the prisoners of anything. Nothing can exist outside time and space in their estimation. Yet it also seems those who believe in a creator, misunderstand the relation of the creator to time and space. They often speak as though God came into existence and quietly slipped into time and space as though it were a glove on his hand.

God the creator is not contained by his creations of time and matter. Time and matter are little more than his footstool. So then how does God see us who are contained within, and trapped by time and space? Consider a person who is watching the sand particles pass through the aperture of an hourglass one by one. Is God limited to only seeing the single grains at a particular point in time? Certainly he is not.

He sees all the grains that have fallen and are yet to fall.

Consider the slide projector analogy. Each slide depicts you at a single moment in your life. The projector only displays one slide at a time and that is how you experience life. But God cannot only see you at any moment, he sees you at all moments in your life, just as if the slides were stacked and he was looking through them from beginning to end.

God *foresees* nothing as he looks at your life. Be sure that his knowledge of all future events does not come from looking at the times of our lives like a tape recording. He does not have to fast-forward or rewind.

God *foreknows* everything in your life because all times are the same for Him. Every time for him is now. He is outside of time and we are prisoners of time. That's why God tells Abraham that his name is 'I Am.' It declares his timeless presence. Just as every moment of your time is now for him, every place in space is present for him because he contains all of space and matter.

Where Is God?

Where then is God if He is outside time? Did he just start up the universe like a clock and allow it to play out only to maybe show up at the end to knock us on the head with justice or mercy?

God is able to be both outside of time and space, and within it. But he is also able to step into time as a part of its stream. This may seem odd, but think what happens when an author or producer writes himself into his own play or movie. This is commonly known among movie directors, but it was original with God.

In Genesis 3:8 Adam and Eve hear the voice of the Lord God walking in the garden. Clearly if the Lord God is the creator of time and space, he is able to enter into it. Isaiah 66:1 declares that heaven is his throne and earth his footstool. Later he would not be just a voice walking, but would enter the world clothed in flesh.

So now consider the original question. How does God attend to the needs and prayers of one man in billions? Quite easily and without any effort once you see that all of time is no time for him.

Within the confines of the laws of nature at any point in time, science has validity, but even then there are limits. For example, we will never be able to assign the result of one divided by zero. The result of division by zero is called infinity and is represented by the symbol ∞. It is a number larger than all other numbers. Contemplating infinity as well as imagining a God outside of time and space simply overwhelms us.

Because God is not traveling with us along a time line, he does not attend to our prayers one after another. He exists in infinity where there is not even a sparrow that falls without his notice. All of a sudden, the question of whether the creative days in Genesis are literal or figurative really doesn't seem to have much importance.

A day with God is no different in time than a thousand years. Though this puzzling inconsistency overwhelms our understanding, let me reassure you that it need not worry or confuse us.

Would we really expect anything less from the one true limitless God?

CHAPTER TWO

That's Not Fair

MY YOUNGEST GRANDSON was just three when out of the blue I heard him say, "*That's not fair!*" His words were emotional and strong. He obviously knew what fair and unfair meant. Having practiced Pediatrics for some thirty years I never stop marveling at this. Children generally develop magical thinking at about age four. Fairness and unfairness, i.e., right and wrong, are concepts far beyond imaginary tea parties with imaginary friends. How did he come to know this concept at age three?

Not only did he have a sense for right and wrong, he assumed that we who were listening had his same understanding for right and wrong. He knew there is a definite line between right and wrong, fair and unfair, and truth and lies.

In all of the animal kingdom, humans are the only species that have this inner understanding called conscience. Animals can be trained to act in a certain way but cannot exhibit true remorse. Conditioned response is not the same as conscientious contemplation.

The Law of Human Nature

It is one thing to say that a small child and his family both relate to the same understanding of right and wrong, but is the concept really universal among all people? What about the sense of right and wrong between nations?

During and since World War II, was there any question of right and wrong between warring nations? C. S. Lewis stated that if Great Britain and Germany didn't have the same sense of right and wrong, the British people could no more blame them for starting the war than for the color of their hair.

What about remote civilizations though? Do you know a country where men would be admired for running away in battle? Is cowardice considered a virtue anywhere? Would a man feel proud of, or be looked up to, for double-crossing all the people who had been kind to him? Remote civilizations within their peoples carry on with a conscience about right and wrong, even within cannibal tribes.

This sense of right and wrong is really more than just conscience though. It is the Law of Human Nature. We humans understand virtue. Good qualities are admired and bad qualities get the squinty eye.

There is no question that the Law of Human Nature is as real as the laws of nature. Everything we do at all times is a reflection of that Law of Human Nature. Within us it does not change. The filter of our person affects the virtues we do or do not exhibit from our inner copy of the Law of Human Nature.

None of us is really keeping the Law of Human Nature. We try to change it to suit our needs. How do we know when we are not keeping it? We began almost immediately to make excuses for ourselves.

Lewis says that we find the Law of Human Nature pressing on us so intensely, that we can't stand to face the fact that we are breaking it. We will do anything to avoid owning up to wrongdoing.

When I was a young Boy Scout, I remember hearing how our

conscience was like a sharp, pointed star. When we did something wrong, the star would begin whirling round and round our heart, pricking it intensely. If we continued to ignore the pricks long enough, the sharp points became dulled. Our conscience would become seared and we could more easily ignore it.

Instincts or Morals

The Law of Human Nature can also be called the Law of Morals or Right Behavior.

Some object to the Law of Human Nature by saying that it is nothing more than instinct. Instincts are natural tendencies, such as the drive for food, or the sexual instinct, or mother love.

Impulses like these are strong desires that are self-centered and are motivated by self-preservation. All animals exhibit instincts.

The Law of Human Nature however allows us to override our instincts.

I read a news article once that told how a man dove off a dam into the water to save a stranger whose daughter had slipped out of their fishing boat but failed to surface. He sustained a broken neck, yet he somehow was still able to rescue the girl. Later he died from the injuries. Similarly it is well known that the firemen who ascended the doomed World Trade Center to rescue strangers knew they would probably not survive. The Law of Human Nature caused the desire to help to overcome the desire for self-preservation on these small and large scales.

Though the Law of Human Nature can act to strengthen one impulse over another, it cannot itself be an instinct. Impulses and instincts never occur out of a sense of right and wrong, fair or unfair.

You might well then suggest that the Law of Human Nature is simply a culturally specific phenomenon. It can be filtered and reflected differently through different cultures, in just the same way that it is filtered through the nature of a single person. I've already explained how the British knew the Nazis were wrong in their unprovoked attacks. What about savage morality compared to civilized morality.

Which one is the 'right' morality? There is not one right culture morality to which we compare all others. The Law of Human Nature exists outside of culture, but is also expressed through each cultural filter.

Each cultural morality is therefore measured against the Law of Human Nature. Everyone and every culture fails to keep the Law of Human Nature. Against what then is cultural morality being measured?

The Religion of Nature

Naturalism is the belief that all that exists is all there ever was or ever will be. There is nothing that preexists.

I've already demonstrated the profound flaws of naturalism when the Laws of Thermodynamics don't line up with astronomical observation. Recently however it has also been thought that there is a part of the universe that is missing. This missing part is called dark matter. And it is not a small amount. Some scientists speculate that it 'makes up' as much as 80% of the universe! It can't be seen, measured, or ascertained by any means, but they believe that it is there!

Naturalists keep producing new ideas to 'fix' the incongruencies between the Laws of Thermodynamics and astronomical observations. But they really don't follow scientific method to do this. An almost philosophic conjecture is shoehorned into what is called scientific method but is really no more than personal belief or bias. This is no more apparent than when scientists drop the word 'theory' from the Theory of Evolution.

This is far outside the bounds of sound science.

Naturalism has evolved into more than a pseudo-science. It is in my opinion a full bore religion. It is on a quest to disprove at all costs the existence of anything before or outside of time and space. Naturalists will not stop there though. If they have their way, nature will eventually control man to the point where it abolishes mankind altogether.[5]

The Law of Human Nature has nothing in common with naturalism. Naturalism is the worship of the creature without recognition of a creator. It renders naturalists incapable of understanding and appreciating nature. Somehow believing that all this came from some soupy volcanic protein pool instead of a creator just doesn't generate as much awe and wonder. The naturalist would simply counter that believers are naive.

Naturalists often put on a party face when it comes to nature. They think that nature is more important than man, so they will preserve it at all costs. Take for example the small three-inch stream-spawning fish called the Delta Smelt in California. Naturalists there would prefer to let drought-stricken farmlands dry up and be lost forever for needed food production and job creation in that state. There are many other similar examples where the naturalist religion is fickle.

Lewis aptly concludes that in nature there are really some things that are more beautiful. Beauty is not just in the eye of the beholder. The biologic mechanism for sight and color cannot explain why a deep orange-red sunset or a summer-shower rainbow are beautiful. God's common grace for an appreciation of nature is the only thing that can account for why we perceive natural beauty. Some things really are more beautiful than others, but there is nothing in the physics or mechanics of nature that cause this. I agree with Lewis and Chamblin that naturalism really doesn't enjoy the beauty of nature, but rather are absorbed in worshipping it.

Think about a clear, dark star-filled sky next time you're out at night. Do your thoughts wander to the balls of hydrogen that make up each and every distant sun or the extreme distances that they must be from Earth? Or do you gaze with awe taking in the beauty of the night sky just as the creator who, when he finished making it, called it all good?

Beyond The Beginning

As I mentioned previously, many scientists begin their discussion of evolution with the primordial soup theory. These warm, rich pools of nutrients somehow developed into proteins that organized into cells that further organized into complex organisms. These organisms then somehow evolved over millions of years into more and more complex organisms. The end result they say, of course, is man.

Because the fossil records don't really show this kind of continuous change, they came up with the theory of interrupted evolution with very fast biologic alterations interrupted by long periods without much variation. Their blind bias excludes any theory of creation which is outside of nature itself.

New scientific hitches will occur which will require these kinds of future revisions and excuses to keep the whole theoretical boat from sinking, no doubt. There is one thing that is certain though. There is no change in the Law of Human Nature. How could that come through the ever-cooking, primordial soup? If it did, then why don't even at least the other higher primates have conscience? They do exhibit conditioned response, but this is not conscience or an understanding of right or wrong.

Without a doubt man had the Law of Human Nature put specifically into him. Certainly this is by no happenstance or by some crazy theory of variation of the primordial soup. If it were variable and from one collection of soup to the next, then it wouldn't be universal, even in man.

The Law of Human Nature points to something beyond and before time and space. Like God it is not of this world. It is inside every one of us and it is hard as nails.

CHAPTER THREE

The Good Force

SO THE LAW OF HUMAN NATURE, also known as the Moral Law, is real. It cannot be explained by anything since the beginning of time and space in nature.

The source had to be outside the universe. The Moral Law was breathed into us, an implant, since the first man, and has been carried somehow through the biologic chain from parents to children.

Whatever Force put it there was present before the universe came into existence. That same Force must have also been the Force that created the universe. Neither the implantation of the Moral Law nor the creation of the universe would be more or less difficult to compare. They are equally inexplicable to us.

Very well then, there must be a creative Force, or we would be the same as all the other animals. The Moral Law cannot be a result of natural changes, culture, habitats, or any kind of evolutionary process.

Good or Bad

For the moment let us suppose then that the Force is some ethereal and non-personal, but all-powerful entity. What we really need to discover is the nature of this Force. Is this Force good or bad?

The distinct, unmistakeable fingerprint of the Force is the Law of Human Nature, or the Moral Law. The Moral Law is about fair and unfair, right and wrong, truth and falsehood. It also is about choosing the right and turning away from the wrong. Our conscience is only pricked with the unfair, the wrong, and the false. That means simply that this Force is the Good Force.

But do both the right and wrong, to which the Moral Law points, come from the Good Force?

It is like bread made with just a little leaven. No part of the loaf is unleavened. Good cannot be sprinkled with a little Bad. Bad spoils all of Good so that no Good remains. There is no such thing as just a little Good or a little Bad. This Force then is either all Good or all Bad.

Where did the Bad Force come from? Was it present before or after the creation?

If it was present before the creation, then it too, like the Good Force, is outside of the universe. The Good Force and the Bad Force would have been coexistent. So consider then that there might have been these two forces outside the universe.

Coexistence of an eternally present Good and Bad presents a question which has to be answered. What makes us call one force good and the other force bad? There are only two possibilities.

Are each of us calling one good and the other bad simply out of our own personal preference or impression of what good and bad is? Do we like one over the other because of the way one makes us feel?

Suppose then that one of these is truly the Good Force and the other the Bad Force and we are not judging them to be so based on our subjective impression. Then there must be a third force that is 'higher up' and 'farther back' than either the Good Force or the Bad Force. That must really be the truly good standard to which the Good Force and Bad Force are being compared. That third force would be the really true Good Force by which we are measuring the other two.

But this result leads back to the original argument. Why do we call that third force good?

Can you see then how that the presence of more than one force prior to the existence of the universe becomes endless, cyclical nonsense? It is meaningless mental gymnastics.

If there were a Good Force and Bad Force eternally existent prior to the creation of the universe, then what we are left with is really just shades of bad. There will really be nothing good.

Very well then, there must be only one Force beyond time and space. The fingerprint of that Force is the Moral Law. The Moral Law which comes from before creation not only tells us fair and unfair, right and wrong, good and bad, but that the Force itself is indeed *all good*.

There is therefore only one entity prior to creation, and that is the Good Force.

The Bad Force

The Bad Force does indeed exist, however. The Moral Law tells us what is right, so there is a wrong. So where did the Bad Force come from?

The Bad Force must have come after the creation of the universe. It must have originated in a created being gone bad. Good must be wholly good and Bad must be wholly bad. But are they equal? Is even our description of good and bad arbitrary?

Again, I contend that the description of good and bad are not arbitrary. They are not equal and not really therefore equal opposites.

Lewis emphatically stated that Bad is a parasite of Good. Bad is always in opposition to Good. Good is prior condition, while Bad is a chosen path of opposition.

But Bad cannot succeed in being bad the way Good does in being good, any more than cowardice can be confused with bravery, or infidelity with faithfulness to a spouse.

Very well then, the Bad Force is the non-preexisting, non-equal opposite of the Good Force.

A Matter of Choice

But why, if the Bad Force is not preexisting, did the Good Force allow it? Surely if the Good Force created everything and implants The Moral Law in man, it has the power to squash the Bad Force?

Yes, the Good Force is just as capable of destroying the Bad Force as it was capable of creating the possibility that led to its existence in the first place. The Good Force is capable also of destroying bad men. It is capable of eliminating all evil everywhere that opposes its settled opposition to its Good-Force nature. Herein is the major crux of the problem of pain and suffering and all that is bad in our world.

If the Good Force were all powerful, then it could make all of creation good. But man is not good. The Moral Law implanted within us tells us that we can, and do, choose bad. So is the Good Force really not all powerful?

Because there is this Moral Law we have a choice between right and wrong. Why did the Good Force allow us to have a choice? If the Good Force had created all things to exist and to act in only good ways, wouldn't that have been better?

That might seem at first preferable. However without choice, would we be any different from mindless, robotic entities with meaningless existence? Without choice, we wouldn't even understand the Moral Law. Without choice there is nothing had that is worth having.

As the Good Force obviously intended to put the Moral Law into the hearts of man even before creation, it is clear that a good choice was always intended as well. Providing choice to man meant that we would not be simple automatonic, mindless beings without purpose or meaning.

Choice definitely means we have purpose and meaning. Giving man a choice is not the act of some ethereal, non-personal entity. It is the act of a very *personal* being. It reveals to us more of the nature of the Good Force.

Creating a world of automated robots would be an act of cruelty from the Bad Force had it existed before the creation of the universe instead of the Good Force. There would be no such thing as the Moral Law in the first place. We would not be even conscious of fair and unfair, right or wrong, good or bad. We would simply exist as mechanical beings devoid of anything called ourself and doing bad things without even the awareness of what bad is.

You can see then, that the Good Force was present before all of creation, is personal and caring, and implants within us *his* Moral Law which allows us to choose to be bad contrary to his nature.

The Good Force must therefore be the personal God. Even more so, God must love us *immensely*. Why else would he give us the freedom to choose?

Predetermination

So God existed before time and space. God is good...all good. God planned to implant his Moral Law into man's heart as part of the plan of creation. God's plan to allow us to choose wrong and not right shows that love is the supreme part of his nature. God is personal.

The Moral Law continues in the heart of all men because God is trying to communicate with each of us. He desires for us to choose right, but loves us enough to allow us to choose wrong.

Now if God existed before and outside time and space, then everything that we do right or wrong is in his 'now.' You might be tempted to argue that this means that he really just created us, and then predetermined our choice of right and wrong.

Remember, he gave us choice. If he had predetermined what we would choose, then did we really have a choice? Why create beings in time and space if you know the choice that they are going to make. Isn't it cruel to create beings whom you will cause to choose wrongly?

This absolutely overwhelms our minds. How could an all-knowing, all-seeing God create man to have choice but yet see the choice that each man would make? Some might argue that existence is then pointless, but you could argue the other side equally as well. Bad means having no choice at all in an existence forever a slave to a cruel master. Good allows a loving relationship for which it is worth existing at all.

It may help to use Lewis' example of trying to understand what a cube is by looking at a drawing of a cube on a flat piece of paper. The paper is two dimensional but the cube is three dimensional. You can draw the cube in many ways and from many perspectives on the paper, but the image depicting the cube on the paper is not itself the cube.

This is a great mystery, but it need not worry and concern us. Would you really expect to fathom all the depths of God in our present state of being? God created us with choice and this is an act of love. This is the very essential nature of God.

God cannot love and at the same time be cruel. Bad can be nothing but cruel and unloving.

CHAPTER FOUR

Our Spiritual Anatomy

EVEN AS A YOUNG CHILD I wanted to know what part of me was heart, spirit, and soul, and how these related to my physical body. What I want to teach you now is your spiritual anatomy. There are three major divisions of your being; your physical body, your soul or heart, and your spirit or mind. Lewis also calls these the belly, the chest, and the head.

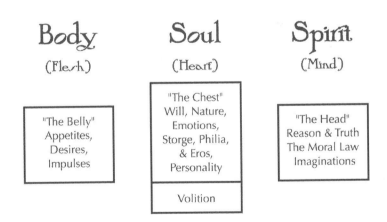

Body (Flesh)	Soul (Heart)	Spirit (Mind)
"The Belly" Appetites, Desires, Impulses	"The Chest" Will, Nature, Emotions, Storge, Philia, & Eros, Personality / Volition	"The Head" Reason & Truth The Moral Law Imaginations

25

Body

In your Flesh resides all your sensual appetites and desires. This is the belly. This is also where your animal instincts reside. This is our common biologic link to all of time and space. The senses of sight, hearing, sensation, taste, and smell all have a direct effect on your body, though they also affect our mind.

When you smell and taste delicious food, your salivary glands produce the necessary saliva to chew and begin digestion. When you hear or see something frightening it revs up your fight or flight response. Sensations are the connection of our body to the physical world around us.

The animal nature of our Flesh has basic needs such as for food, space, sexual intercourse, etc. This animal nature drives us to meet all of its needs and wants. To see the Flesh in action, one only needs to watch the daily activities of a mother with a baby. Most all of the needs that she meets are needs of the baby's Flesh.

Our Flesh is the visible and physical connection that we have with time and space. It is our common link to all the other animals in the world.

Soul

In the Soul, also known as your Heart, resides the personality that is ourself. All that is you resides here in the chest, the seat of magnanimity or greatness. Primarily this is your will, your emotions, and the source of the three loves called storge, philia, and eros.

Storge is human love such as would be experienced by a mother nursing her baby, or a father wrestling playfully in the floor with a young son. It is affectionate love.

Philia is the non-physical love between friends and is the most

26

spiritual of the three. While storge usually has a biological bond or association, philia does not. The affection between friends is not a physical love at all, but rather a bond of mutual agreement. Friends are friends out of a mutual enjoyment of the other's company.

Eros comprises romantic love. Erotic or sexual affection is part of, but not the same as eros. Romantic love often begins with physical attraction, but mature eros grows far beyond just that.

Most importantly, all of our actions, i.e., our volitions, come through the Heart before they materialize. Volition is our will expressed. All that comes out of us that is good or bad, proceeds from the act of our will. The Soul is the place of our personality. It is also the seat of a depraved human nature.

Spirit

Your Mind, or your Spirit, is your head. It is the seat of your reason, i.e., your thinking ability.

It is where you keep a copy of truth, as you know it. Your reasoning ability considers everything that comes into it against your copy of the truth. The Law of Human Nature resides here too.

Your truth and the real truth may be different. We all jade our copy of truth to some extent in order to benefit ourselves. This is also part of why mankind is utterly depraved. The Law of Human Nature is like a prism through which your copy of truth passes. It compares your truth to real truth, then pokes you with your conscience. If your conscience has become worn and seared, then the pricks and pokes are just dull nudges that you learn to ignore.

This is where imagination incubates as well. These are imaginations of all things, good and bad, vain or provident.

Breath of God

The obvious questions are how these parts came to be, and what will happen to them beyond the end of biologic life.

The Bible provides the account of creation which says that the animals were created before man. No doubt their physical bodies were formed from the earth just as man's. Beyond that though, God does something different. He breathed into man His own breath of life. Now it does not say he did the same thing with the other animals. It suggests to me that this was when God put the spirit and soul, the mind and the heart, into mankind. And it is important to note that this is what really distinguishes us from all other animals.

The very breath of God that gives us spirit and soul also breathes into us his Moral Law, The Law of Human Nature.

When God finished creating he made an amazing and very important statement. He proclaimed that everything he created was good. This was his stamp of authenticity, the mark of his very hand on mankind.

At this point there was nothing spoiled in all of the natural creation. Mankind contained no hint of depravity.

CHAPTER FIVE

Virtue and Vice

THE INTERACTIONS BETWEEN the three major parts of our spiritual anatomy are very important. From these interactions everything becomes a volitional act of our will, whether good or bad. When virtue rules over vice, the outward manifestations are the external qualities of Matthew 5:3-13.

The Seven Deadly Sins

Dorothy Sayers is well known for her treatise on *The Other Six Deadly Sins*[6] as well as her translation and commentary on all of the deadly sins in the Penguin edition of Dante's *Divine Comedy*.[7]

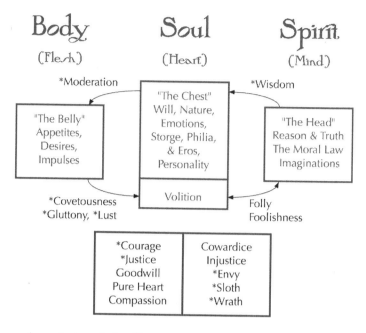

Body
(Flesh)

Soul
(Heart)

Spirit
(Mind)

*Moderation

*Wisdom

"The Chest"
Will, Nature,
Emotions,
Storge, Philia,
& Eros,
Personality

"The Belly"
Appetites,
Desires,
Impulses

"The Head"
Reason & Truth
The Moral Law
Imaginations

*Covetousness
*Gluttony, *Lust

Volition

Folly
Foolishness

*Courage	Cowardice
*Justice	Injustice
Goodwill	*Envy
Pure Heart	*Sloth
Compassion	*Wrath

The seven foundational deadly sins are listed below. I'm going to spend considerable time on Pride so I won't touch on that here other than to say that is the foundational sin from which all the other sins spring. All of the deadly sins are perversions. These are root sins to which all acts of sin spring.

The Seven Deadly Sins
1. Pride
2. Envy
3. Wrath
4. Sloth
5. Covetousness
6. Gluttony
7. Lust

Envy is the perverted desire for your own good which motivates you to deprive others of their good. The focus of envy is not simply an object. It is generalized disdain for all good in someone else.

30

Covetousness, or avarice, though somewhat similar, is not the same as envy. Covetousness is the pervasive desire for something that someone else has, while avarice is the love of money and power.

Wrath is a perverted love of justice that causes one to pursue spiteful revenge. God's wrath however is not a perversion because it is the settled opposition of his holy nature to all that is evil.[8] His wrath never comes out of any desire to get even but is based on his never-erring justice. Our wrath is self-serving vengeance while his wrath is the absolute and perfect measure of perfect justice. The source of his wrath is not out of an emotional response like ours.

Sloth is indifference, i.e., the failure to love any good object. It rises further than simple laziness. It is the conscious indifference to God's will. It is a man's inner voice which says to God 'Whatever!'

Gluttony, for most people, is often associated with food, but it is really far worse. It is the perverted love of pleasure. Lest you think yourself immune from this, consider all the things that you enjoy in your life. If you have deep-seated cravings for anything that steers your actions like the rudder of a ship, then you have a perverted desire for pleasure.

Lust is the perverted love of persons. Interestingly this is not just limited to eros or erotic love. Lust can also be present within storge and philia. Lewis gives a quite common example of lust within storge in The Great Divorce[9] and idolatrous lust can occur within the marriage relationship unfortunately.[10]

Four Cardinal Virtues

Here we will talk about the interactions of vice and virtue within our spiritual anatomy.

There are four cardinal virtues, so-called because they are pivotal. There are three theological virtues that I will discuss later. The Latin word for cardinal originates from 'the hinge of a door.' These cardinal virtues have throughout time been recognized across multiple cultures and all civilized people, as well.

The Four Cardinal Virtues
1. Wisdom
2. Moderation or Temperance
3. Courage
4. Justice or Keeping Promises

The Lord Jesus Christ's very words in Matthew 5:3-13 tell us what the hallmarks of a whole man are. This is a section of scripture known as the Beatitudes. We tend to scan over these quickly when reading them, but you should recognize that many of these are direct opposites of the seven deadly sins. You should study these closely because they are very important measures to size yourself up.

Matthew 5:3 Blessed are the poor in spirit, for theirs is the kingdom of heaven. 4 Blessed are those who mourn, for they will be comforted. 5 Blessed are the meek, for they will inherit the earth. 6 Blessed are those who hunger and thirst for righteousness, for they will be filled. 7 Blessed are the merciful, for they will be shown mercy. 8 Blessed are the pure in heart, for they will see God. 9 Blessed are the peacemakers, for they will be called sons of God. 10 Blessed are those who are persecuted because of righteousness, for theirs is the kingdom of heaven. 11 Blessed are you when people insult you, persecute you and falsely say all kinds of evil against you because of me. 12 Rejoice and be glad, because great is your reward in heaven, for in the same way they persecuted the prophets who were before you. 13 You are the salt of the earth. But if the salt loses its saltiness, how can it be made salty again? It is no longer good for anything, except to be thrown out and trampled by men.

Wisdom occurs when our Reason apprehends Truth and then governs our Will. Our Heart receives Wisdom and then our Volition acts accordingly. This results in Courage, Justice, Goodwill, a Pure Heart, and Compassion. Moderation occurs when our Heart then overrules any Flesh desires or impulses.

Courage is the testing point of all the other virtues. Justice is the evidence and results of Courage. Chivalry is the combination of Courage and Justice with the personality trait of gentleness.

How you Reason, is terribly important as Proverbs 23:7 clearly states.

Proverbs 23:7 For as he thinketh in his heart, so is he: Eat and
drink, saith he to thee; but his heart is not with thee.

When your Reason, i.e., your Intellect, becomes dark or downcast, you cannot apprehend Truth. Your Will and Volition produce Cowardice, Injustice, Envy, Sloth, or Wrath. Attacks on the mind are specifically intended to darken the intellect for this very reason.[11] The effect cascades dramatically and disastrously as 2 Corinthians 4:4 shows.

2 Corinthians 4:4 In whom the god of this world hath blinded the
minds of them which believe not, lest the light of the glorious
gospel of Christ, who is the image of God, should shine unto
them.

Vain imaginations directly affect both Truth and Reason which also serves to darken the intellect as described in Romans 1:21. This darkening can affect the Heart as well.

Romans 1:21 Because that, when they knew God, they glorified him not as God, neither were thankful; but became vain in their imaginations, and their foolish heart was darkened.

Now you might have wondered why I show Volition in its own compartment. All sin that comes out of our Volition leaves black marks on our soul. Once a black mark is present we cannot erase or cover it. The process of interaction between Reason, Truth, and Will occurs instantly and there is certainly interaction. What happens when you think bad thoughts? Do they instantly become these black marks? Mark 7:15 is quite clear here.

> *Mark 7:15* There is nothing from without a man, that entering into him can defile him: but the things which come out of him, those are they that defile the man.

Thoughts constantly flow into our Reason and we instantly reference it against Truth. At that moment we have the opportunity to discard it. If we don't discard it, we can deposit it into our Imagination where we may revisit it, even repeatedly obsess on it time after time. If it is a vain Imagination and we revisit it, we can alter our copy of Truth. Folly and Foolishness rather than Wisdom is then injected into our Will. In our Heart, the vain imagination becomes an act of our Volition and produces sin, a black mark on our soul.

It is critical that we actively take every thought captive as stated in 2 Corinthians 10:5. Even more though we need to actively nurture good thoughts according to Philippians 4:8.

> *2 Corinthians 10:5* Casting down imaginations, and every high thing that exalteth itself against the knowledge of God, and bringing into captivity every thought to the obedience of Christ;

> *Phillipians 4:8* Finally, brethren, whatsoever things are true, whatsoever things are honest, whatsoever things are just,

whatsoever things are pure, whatsoever things are lovely, whatsoever things are of good report; if there be any virtue, and if there be any praise, think on these things.

When Reason apprehends Truth, the Will governs and overrules the Belly. Moderation, i.e., Temperance, must constantly throttle the impulses and desires of our Flesh. It is important to understand that desires for food, sex, etc., have a legitimate presence in our Flesh. Remember when God created Man, he said it was good. He has provided a way for those desires to be met in a legitimate way, but he never intended us to be ruled by the Belly.

Controlling desires of the Flesh starts in the Spirit. We certainly must take every thought captive so we can moderate the Flesh, or Covetousness, Gluttony, or Lust results. However, there are times when certain of these desires must be encouraged and fanned such as in the marriage bed. A husband and a wife have a duty to encourage and fan healthy sexual impulses toward each other, since marriage of the two is culminated in that physical connection. Paul is very clear in 1 Corinthians 7:1-9.

1 Corinthians 7:1 Now concerning the things whereof ye wrote unto me: It is good for a man not to touch a woman. 2 Nevertheless, to avoid fornication, let every man have his own wife, and let every woman have her own husband. 3 Let the husband render unto the wife due benevolence: and likewise also the wife unto the husband. 4 The wife hath not power of her own body, but the husband: and likewise also the husband hath not power of his own body, but the wife. 5 Defraud ye not one the other, except it be with consent for a time, that ye may give yourselves to fasting and prayer; and come together again, that Satan tempt you not for your incontinency. 6 But I speak this by permission, and not of commandment. 7 For I would that all men were even as I myself. But every man hath his proper gift of God, one after this manner, and another after that. [8] I say therefore to the unmarried and widows, It is good for them if they abide even as I. [9] But if they cannot contain, let them marry: for it is better to marry than to burn.

All the cardinal virtues as well as the deadly sins have a presence within us and an expression outside of us. What we say and do that results in a volitional expression of any sin leaves a black mark on our soul. It is that black mark that cannot be erased, even when the offended person has granted forgiveness. Our words echo in testimony against us forever.

But there is another black mark whose presence is not caused by any volitional act. It is the black mark of human depravity. The black marks of our individual selves prove its existence. We are utterly fallen creatures, seduced and captured by temptation in the first place. We suffer from a sinful nature which is the source of our depravity and from sin that we commit.

We could perhaps decide to continually do better until we come to a place where we can control most all of the volitional sins. But what do we do about the black marks we have already accumulated?

And even more, what about the black mark of our human depravity? We can never fix that ourselves.

CHAPTER SIX

Three Personalities

SO WE HAVE A DIRE DILEMMA.

God our creator, put within us his Moral Law. His nature is all good. His nature is only good. If we followed his Moral Law perfectly, we would be good too.

Adam and Eve's first failure to keep the Moral Law doomed all of their descendants to the Black Mark of mankind's depraved nature. They, and each individual descended from them, also started their own individual collection of Black Marks. The Black Mark and the Black Marks persist even to this day for all of us.

What could God do? Is there any way out of this dilemma. Could it be that he didn't see this coming?

God Is Love

Genesis 22:1 And it came to pass after these things, that God did
tempt Abraham, and said unto him, Abraham: and he said,
Behold, here I am. 2 And he said, Take now thy son, thine only
son Isaac, whom thou lovest, and get thee into the land of
Moriah; and offer him there for a burnt offering upon one of

the mountains which I will tell thee of.

3 And Abraham rose up early in the morning, and saddled his ass, and took two of his young men with him, and Isaac his son, and clave the wood for the burnt offering, and rose up, and went unto the place of which God had told him. 4 Then on the third day Abraham lifted up his eyes, and saw the place afar off.

5 And Abraham said unto his young men, Abide ye here with the ass; and I and the lad will go yonder and worship, and come again to you. 6 And Abraham took the wood of the burnt offering, and laid it upon Isaac his son; and he took the fire in his hand, and a knife; and they went both of them together.

7 And Isaac spake unto Abraham his father, and said, My father: and he said, Here am I, my son. And he said, Behold the fire and the wood: but where is the lamb for a burnt offering?

8 And Abraham said, My son, God will provide himself a lamb for a burnt offering: so they went both of them together.

9 And they came to the place which God had told him of; and Abraham built an altar there, and laid the wood in order, and bound Isaac his son, and laid him on the altar upon the wood. 10 And Abraham stretched forth his hand, and took the knife to slay his son.

11 And the angel of the LORD called unto him out of heaven, and said, Abraham, Abraham: and he said, Here am I. 12 And he said, Lay not thine hand upon the lad, neither do thou any thing unto him: for now I know that thou fearest God, seeing thou hast not withheld thy son, thine only son from me. 13 And Abraham lifted up his eyes, and looked, and behold behind him a ram caught in a thicket by his horns: and Abraham went and

took the ram, and offered him up for a burnt offering in the stead of his son. 14 And Abraham called the name of that place Jehovah jireh: as it is said to this day, In the mount of the LORD it shall be seen.

Perichoresis[12] is a term derived from a Greek word. It is also known as *circumincession* or *circuminsession*. The image that comes to my mind is the swirling contents of a mixing bowl. As the contents spiral inward to the middle they eventually fold under only to emerge near the rim to begin the inward spiral all over again.

God is agape love, i.e., the kind of love that God has for us. Each of the three persons of God loves the other two. Each of the three persons of God receives love from the others. Perichoresis is the infolding of God's love like the contents of that mixing bowl.

There is God the Father, God the Son, and God the Holy Spirit. Our concept of love implies its exchange between at least two. That is the way we understand love. The Trinity is a mystery described by God to us in the best way we can comprehend it. God the Father loves God the Son. They each love God the Holy Spirit and the Holy Spirit loves them. Each gives love and each returns love. God the Holy Spirit is the bond of love between God the Father and God the Son. Agape love *requires* the bonded trinity.

God the Son is the only begotten Son, the Word of God. By the Word of God, Adam was created. By Adam we were begotten. God the Son is like God the Father just as we are like Adam, our father.

We were created in the image of God, not to be Gods, or because God needed us. We were created out of the overflowing abundance of his perichoretic love. Worship in our heart is much like perichoresis. It is repeatedly infolded and emerges as enjoyment which is then folded into further worship. We not only enjoy our worship, we worship God *by* enjoying him forever. This is God's great gift to us.

So if God loved us, why did he create us even though he knew that we would fail?

God, who is outside of time, is never taken by surprise. He has always had a plan. Early in Genesis the story of Abraham and Isaac reveals his plan. When Abraham says that God will provide himself a sacrifice, I read that as *God will provide himself as the sacrifice*. Abraham is a *type or shadow* of all mankind just as Isaac is a *type or shadow* of God the Son.

God the Son takes on the flesh of mankind and becomes the Son of man. God the Holy Spirit raises the body of the Son of man from the dead. The risen Son of man stands before God the Father declaring that we are made innocent. *All* of our black marks are not then just covered —they are gone! But there is something deeper here worth understanding better.

The settled nature of God's holiness requires absolute justice. But the settled nature of God's love requires mercy. He didn't just let us off! God the Father metes out pure justice that our sin requires to God the Son. God the Son extends pure mercy to us by accepting the justice of what was our due reward. God the Holy Spirit binds the three of them together, because God *is* agape love.

God is God and he *never* changes. He is the same in time now as he was before we were created. You can see why I say mercy kisses justice, and we who truly believe are saved. Though it seems superfluous to say it, until we ask to be saved, we are truly therefore lost.

John 3:16 For God so loved the world that he gave his only begotten
    son, that whosoever believeth on him should not perish, but
    have everlasting life. 17 He that believeth on him is not
    condemned: but he that believeth not is condemned already,
    because he hath not believed in the name of the only begotten
    Son of God.

Black Marks

Luke 19:10 For the Son of man is come to seek and to save that
which was lost.

It is profound that God would provide himself a sacrifice by providing
himself to *be* that sacrifice. But why and how can that be?

The one big Black Mark we all get for having Adam as our father is
passed from generation to generation throughout all time. Even if
anyone along the way lived a life so as not to accumulate any other
Black Marks from acts of sin, there would always be that one big Black
Mark.

In order for a person to stand as a sacrifice in the place of all
mankind, that person could have no Black Marks of either kind. Before
God we stand guilty, but only standing before him can we be cured. We
cannot do with God, and we cannot do without him. Lewis states that
he is our supreme terror and our supreme need.

Beyond being convinced that God the Father loves you, and wants
to redeem you, how can you be sure that God the Son became the Son
of man in the person of Jesus of Nazareth? Even John the Baptist
appeared later in his ministry to question the deity of Jesus. Jesus is
absolutely clear about who he is. No one, *especially not a Jew*, has ever
talked the way Jesus did. The forgiveness he granted is the *sole* domain
of God.

Luke 7:19 And John calling unto him two of his disciples sent them
to Jesus, saying, Art thou he that should come? or look we for
another? 20 When the men were come unto him, they said, John
Baptist hath sent us unto thee, saying, Art thou he that should
come? or look we for another? 21 And in that same hour he

cured many of their infirmities and plagues, and of evil spirits; and unto many that were blind he gave sight. 22 Then Jesus answering said unto them, Go your way, and tell John what things ye have seen and heard; how that the blind see, the lame walk, the lepers are cleansed, the deaf hear, the dead are raised, to the poor the gospel is preached. 23 And blessed is he, whosoever shall not be offended in me.

Luke 5:24 But that ye may know that the Son of man hath power upon earth to forgive sins, (he said unto the sick of the palsy,) I say unto thee, Arise, and take up thy couch, and go into thine house.

Jesus' words of forgiveness continued right through a tortuous beating and up onto the cross. Even at the point of death, Jesus is actively forgiving. His purpose was always forgiveness. He is the only way to cure mankind. He even stands between us and our transgressors and forgives them without our permission. His authority to forgive our transgressors is the same reason he can forgive our transgressions.

Jesus Christ doesn't need our permission to forgive because he is the party chiefly wounded by all sin.

Luke 23:32 And there were also two other, malefactors, led with him to be put to death. 33 And when they were come to the place, which is called Calvary, there they crucified him, and the malefactors, one on the right hand, and the other on the left. 34 Then said Jesus, Father, forgive them; for they know not what they do. And they parted his raiment, and cast lots. 35 And the people stood beholding. And the rulers also with them derided him, saying, He saved others; let him save himself, if he be Christ, the chosen of God.

Luke 19:10 For the Son of man is come to seek and to save that which was lost.

Jesus was absolutely clear about his authority, and not just to forgive sin. He alone has the power to give up his life. No one could take it from him. When he was hanging on the cross, his death was not a consequence of the life slowly ebbing from his body as I had long thought. Jesus could not die until he uttered the words commanding his body to give up its life.

> *John 10:17* Therefore doth my Father love me, because I lay down my life, that I might take it again. 18 No man taketh it from me, but I lay it down of myself. I have power to lay it down, and I have power to take it again. This commandment have I received of my Father.

> *Luke 23:44* And it was about the sixth hour, and there was a darkness over all the earth until the ninth hour. 45 And the sun was darkened, and the veil of the temple was rent in the midst. 46 And when Jesus had cried with a loud voice, he said, Father, into thy hands I commend my spirit: and having said thus, he gave up the ghost.

The red thread of God's love for us is captured by both his nature of justice and mercy. Justice for sin must occur because of his settled holiness. At the same time, it is fully his nature to extend love and mercy. When God the Son presents his own blood before God the Father, mercy kisses justice. No one else but God the Son can do this for man. We didn't just get off the hook. We have been bought with a price. You can see now why Lewis writes the following.

> *"I am trying here to prevent anyone saying the really foolish thing that people often say about Him: 'I'm ready to accept Jesus as a great moral teacher, but I don't accept His claim to be God.' That is the one*

thing we must not say. A man who was merely a man and said the sort of things Jesus said would not be a great moral teacher. He would either be a lunatic—on a level with the man who says he is a poached egg—or else he would be the Devil of Hell. You must make your choice. Either this man was, and is, the Son of God: or else a madman or something worse. You can shut Him up for a fool, you can spit at Him and kill Him as a demon; or you can fall at His feet and call Him Lord and God. But let us not come with any patronising nonsense about His being a great human teacher. He has not left that open to us. He did not intend to." -C.S. Lewis[13]

Either Jesus is God the Son–the Son of man–or he is a lunatic or a devil. There is no other choice. If he is your hope, then there is no power in the universe that can take you from him, and no Black Mark that can remain.

If he is not your hope, then you have locked him out. Jesus says in Mathew 16:18 that upon himself will he build the church and that the gates of hell shall not prevail against it. To reject Jesus Christ as the risen Son of God is to lock yourself within the gates of yourself. Hell is truly locked from the inside.

It can never infect our Heaven.

CHAPTER SEVEN

The First Black Mark

Isaiah 14:12 How art thou fallen from heaven, O Lucifer, son of the
morning! how art thou cut down to the ground, which didst
weaken the nations! 13 For thou hast said in thine heart, I will
ascend into heaven, I will exalt my throne above the stars of
God: I will sit also upon the mount of the congregation, in the
sides of the north: 14 I will ascend above the heights of the
clouds; I will be like the most High. 15 Yet thou shalt be brought
down to hell, to the sides of the pit. 16 They that see thee shall
narrowly look upon thee, and consider thee, saying, Is this the
man that made the earth to tremble, that did shake kingdoms;
17 That made the world as a wilderness, and destroyed the cities
thereof; that opened not the house of his prisoners? 18 All the
kings of the nations, even all of them, lie in glory, every one in
his own house. 19 But thou art cast out of thy grave like an
abominable branch, and as the raiment of those that are slain,
thrust through with a sword, that go down to the stones of the
pit; as a carcase trodden under feet. 20 Thou shalt not be joined
with them in burial, because thou hast destroyed thy land, and
slain thy people: the seed of evildoers shall never be renowned.

Luke 10:17 And the seventy returned again with joy, saying, Lord, even the devils are subject unto us through thy name. 18 And he said unto them, I beheld Satan as lightning fall from heaven. 19 Behold, I give unto you power to tread on serpents and scorpions, and over all the power of the enemy: and nothing shall by any means hurt you. 20 Notwithstanding in this rejoice not, that the spirits are subject unto you; but rather rejoice, because your names are written in heaven.

PRIDE IS THE ROOT SIN. Out of it springs all the other six deadly sins. Pride was the first Black Mark and Lucifer succumbed to it because he wanted to be God. With all the might and power of this created being, he became the most evil because he gave himself wholly to Pride.

Pride is the most serious Black Mark that faces a Christian. Pride was what caused Adam and Eve to sin in the first place. Pride was the beginning of mankind's generational Black Mark, the one that you and I carry until our death. Without accepting Jesus Christ's forgiveness, that Black Mark will be there for all of time. For created beings, time will always exist. God created us for time and space.

Proverbs 16:18 Pride goeth before destruction, and an haughty spirit before a fall.

Pride is what tricks us into believing the lie. Adam and Eve believed the lie. And they too wanted to be like God.

Genesis 3:1 Now the serpent was more subtil than any beast of the field which the LORD God had made. And he said unto the woman, Yea, hath God said, Ye shall not eat of every tree of the garden? 2 And the woman said unto the serpent, We may eat of the fruit of the trees of the garden: 3 But of the fruit of the tree which is in the midst of the garden, God hath said, Ye shall not

46

eat of it, neither shall ye touch it, lest ye die. 4 And the serpent said unto the woman, Ye shall not surely die: 5 For God doth know that in the day ye eat thereof, then your eyes shall be opened, and ye shall be as gods, knowing good and evil.

Unforgiveness is pure pride. God forgives as though he is the wounded party in all sin. We attempt to hold God hostage by refusing to forgive so that we can exact our wrath on another person. We may as well stand shaking our fist in his face. God will not only resist us, but he will hold us accountable for our sins. It is utter foolishness. Forgiveness is the central fabric of Christianity.

> *Mark 11:25* And when ye stand praying, forgive, if ye have ought against any: that your Father also which is in heaven may forgive you your trespasses. 26 But if ye do not forgive, neither will your Father which is in heaven forgive your trespasses.

> *James 4:6* But he giveth more grace. Wherefore he saith, God resisteth the proud, but giveth grace unto the humble.

Christians will struggle with Pride all of the days of this life. It is Satan's primary weapon against us. Pride assaults Truth and if it succeeds in changing our copy of Truth, then Reason will not govern our Will. Our Will and our Belly will instead rule our Spirit and the end result will be Folly and Foolishness.

Does God have Pride?

Jesus Christ tells his disciples to learn of him for he is lowly and humble. God has no pride. It is not in his nature. He simply has no need for it. He is not trying to impress anyone or anything. He needs no strokes from anyone to hold up an ego, nor does he revel in power.

I remember going to a children's outreach event held at the local theatre in the small town where I was born and raised. I don't remember much about the evangelist, but I will never forget how he taught us to pray using the acronym PRAY.

'P' stands for praise. That is always the first thing that you do when you approach God. Why is that? Does God need our praise?

No, he doesn't. God has no pride to stroke and he is dependent on no one and nothing.

He tells us to Praise him because it is good for *us*. Praise not only enfolds us into God's perichoretic love, it assaults our Pride against which it has no defense. Praise causes humility to rise within us.

So where does Praise come from? It comes from Faith, Hope, and Love which the Holy Spirit binds to our Heart. Just as the Holy Spirit is there to bind us to God the Father and God the Son, he binds each of us to the three persons of God.

In Matthew 12:31 Jesus says that whoever speaks a word against the Holy Spirit, it will not be forgiven ever. He further states in Mark 3:29 that whoever blasphemes the Holy Spirit is in danger of eternal damnation. This caused me no small amount of disquiet as a young boy wondering about this unforgivable sin.

Once you understand that God the Holy Spirit is what binds you to God the Trinity, this makes perfect sense. The only sin that God can't forgive is the one you won't confess to him. When you refuse to confess that sin, what you are doing is telling the Holy Spirit to leave you alone. Without the Holy Spirit binding Faith, Hope, and Love to your heart, you cannot partake of Jesus Christ's saving act.

The Holy Spirit is every bit God. Just as you need to think of Jesus Christ as no mere man, but absolute God with human flesh, you must understand that God the Holy Spirit is with you, under you, by you, and before and after you. He is a member of the three personal God.

So Praise brings humility and assaults Pride, but does it do more? Praise is worship we should enjoy. Remember how I told you that we worship God *by* enjoying him!

'R' stands for repentance. Until the moment we are changed at the last trumpet, we will always struggle with vile evil thoughts. Simply thinking a bad thought does not mean you have sinned. It is true of course that as a man thinks in his heart, so is he. But the thought becomes sin when we express it as a volitional act of our will.

> *2 Corinthians 10:3* For though we walk in the flesh, we do not war after the flesh: 4 (For the weapons of our warfare are not carnal, but mighty through God to the pulling down of strong holds;) 5 Casting down imaginations, and every high thing that exalteth itself against the knowledge of God, and bringing into captivity every thought to the obedience of Christ; 6 And having in a readiness to revenge all disobedience, when your obedience is fulfilled.

Clearly our battle is in the mind where we alone hold the key. We have the opportunity to ride roughshod over evil thoughts within ourselves and prevent Black Marks. Because we are human and our nature is still depraved, we will have failures. Black Marks will happen. Those Black Marks will not loosen the Holy Spirit's binding on our heart. Praise leads to repentance and the Holy Spirit sees to it that our heart's cries come before God the Father and God the Son.

Matthew 13 relates how the Word is received by different people. When the Word is planted in us we receive it as Truth. Our Reason apprehends it and presents it to our Heart. If our Heart accepts it at first, but the Truth is stolen away, such that anything growing in our Heart withers, then we will stand before God as with only filthy rags and foul breath.

Once that Word is planted and the Heart accepts it, the Holy Spirit binds Faith, Hope, and Love to us and begins the work of cleaning and clothing us. That process will only end when in that one final dramatic change he removes from us the possibility to apprehend anything but Truth. We will then never be able to sin because our nature will have been forever changed.

Repentance means that until that final change, we come with the humility that praise brings, and confess those sins that we have committed and ask for strength to cast down the thoughts which lead to them.

'A' stands for anyone. Pray for anyone and everyone.

As humans we are drawn to both surface area and to form. We measure our very life by surface area and we value lots of things by a square unit of measure.

Form is the attractiveness of a thing or person. We can be inwardly moved to think and do things by the form of a beautiful woman, a handsome man, a sporty car, fine jewelry, a luxurious house, etc. Our attachment to form must be overcome since we tend to judge everything by how pleasing it is to look at or how much we think it will meet some need in ourselves.

When we pray for others, we need to be very careful to avoid the traps of surface area and form. You would be very wrong to think of beautiful people more than you ought, and unattractive people less than you should. Remember when you look at people, that you are seeing who they are at this point in time. You are not seeing who they will be when they are finally changed. Some people are going to be sorely disappointed or equally startled by the changes that God works in us. It is quite possible they might not even recognize those people in heaven at first glance!

We need to grasp that we are creatures of time and space and we always will be. We need to remember God will complete what he has begun in each of us. Of the four loves, only agape love stands above and beyond spoilage. Storge, philia, and eros can all be turned to evil, selfish purposes.

50

'Y' of course stands for yourself.

This is not where you should be praying for things per se. As a young child or new Christian that is always where we start. We are told to present our petitions to God the Father. As we grow and mature, we realize just how selfish our prayers are at the start and how much more mature they become. I am thankful for the petty prayers that weren't answered because many of them would have done me harm.

Our character pluses and minuses become the object of prayer about ourself. The binding nature of the Holy Spirit gently urges us on. We come to regret our shortcomings, long and strive for improvements. Children's wishful prayers for things like bicycles and such become prayers to be good fathers and mothers and people of character.

I'm not saying that if you are praying for things that you are in the wrong. You will grow to long for better things though, and that is worth looking forward to.

Three Theological Virtues

Hebrews 11:1 Now faith is the substance of things hoped for, the evidence of things not seen. 2 For by it the elders obtained a good report. 3 Through faith we understand that the worlds were framed by the word of God, so that things which are seen were not made of things which do appear.

John 6:44 No man can come to me, except the Father which hath sent me draw him: and I will raise him up at the last day.

By the merit of the common grace that God gives to all men, everyone can grasp the four cardinal virtues; wisdom, temperance, courage, and justice.

The three theological virtues are particular to Christianity. They can only be installed in our Heart if we believe on and accept forgiveness from Jesus Christ who is God the Son. Faith and Hope and Love are intimately connected. No one has any real hope beyond that Hope.

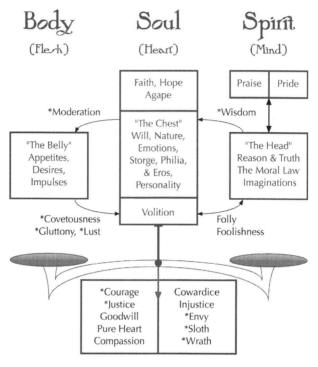

When our Spirit 'hears' that there is hope for our sad condition, it is God's call to our hearts. But Hope comes after God's calling and God's calling is strong, very strong. In John 6:44, the word translated 'draw' carries the sense of 'drag.' God's calling is essentially dragging you to see Truth.

When our Reason apprehends the unadulterated Truth of God, then our Heart is faced with the decision of accepting or rejecting Christ. The only way that we can reject Christ is to lock him out. Immediately if we accept Christ, the seed of Faith is planted in our heart. Faith blooms as Christ's Love causes Hope to grow. The Holy Spirit then binds to our heart Faith and Hope with Agape Love.

Faith leads to Hope, Hope brings Love, from Love springs the fountain of Praise, and Praise assaults our Pride. It makes us to stand upright in the presence of God with clean garments and fresh breath, free of the stench of our foul depraved nature. We can no longer be assaulted by the enemy. There are no footholds in our life and so we can join in that swirling circumincession of God's Love.

CHAPTER EIGHT

The First Wedding

Genesis 2:21 And the LORD God caused a deep sleep to fall upon
Adam, and he slept: and he took one of his ribs, and closed up
the flesh instead thereof; 22 And the rib, which the LORD God
had taken from man, made he a woman, and brought her unto
the man. 23 And Adam said, This is now bone of my bones, and
flesh of my flesh: she shall be called Woman, because she was
taken out of Man. 24 Therefore shall a man leave his father and
his mother, and shall cleave unto his wife: and they shall be one
flesh. 25 And they were both naked, the man and his wife, and
were not ashamed.

I'VE DESCRIBED TO YOU already how science describes the
inexplicable beginning of space and time from a single point, out of
nothing, and in a blaze of heat. From a theological perspective however
it begins with God himself who is outside of time and space and
without a beginning.

He creates the heavens and the earth which were initially formless
amid the void of space and commands light to come forth. The first day
ends. God pronounces that creation is good. The second day he divides
the waters of the atmosphere from the waters of the oceans. Dry land

and vegetation appear on the third day. The stars and the moon are created to shine into space on the fourth day. The fifth day, God creates the fishes and the fowl. On the sixth day he creates all the land animals. And each time, God pronounces it good.

Whether these days are literal days as we know them, prophetic timetables, or large spans of time are actually of little importance. In the first place, a day with the Lord is no different from a thousand years simply because he does not travel along the timeline of all that he has created. In the second place, his descriptions of each of the creative days is just as overwhelming as is the description of the trinity.

Just because it overwhelms us does not mean that it need concern us. It most definitely cannot detract from the accuracy of the description. In reality how could you compare what someone might claim scientifically about creation when you are aware of the very limited understanding science has about that subject anyway?

On the sixth day he creates something different. He creates man and then woman, but he creates them in his own image. I think that the image may well not just be a physical image, but that of the triune nature of God. He gave man a Spirit, a Soul, and a Body. And he created us to be always with him.

After God created man, he anesthetized him in a deep sleep, and bone and marrow were extracted. From Adams own flesh God created woman and he did so in such a way that they could carry mankind on. Adam begets sons and daughters through Eve who is the mother of them all. The only difference is one little Y chromosome in Adam.

Then God himself presents Eve to Adam. This was the very first wedding.

I actually enjoy weddings. The appearance of the bride beautifully adorned and clothed in the purity of white is refreshing and renewing. As a Pediatrician, I do get excited about parents and newborns. Families are the incubators of human life that begin with a man and woman.

Why did God create man and woman in this way, though?

Figura Umbrae

Figura umbrae is latin for the shape of the shadow. I told you earlier about how together Abraham and Isaac were a type and shadow of mankind and God the Son. The Bible is steeped with *figura umbrae*. God often uses them to illustrate things of importance, and to show us insight and understanding into his mind. I think of it as his way of flagging certain scripture with "Pay attention! This will help you."

The different way that God created man and woman from all other animals is perhaps one of the most significant. What does it mean?

> *Matthew 19:4.* And he answered and said unto them, Have ye not read, that he which made them at the beginning made them male and female, 5 And said, For this cause shall a man leave father and mother, and shall cleave to his wife: and they twain shall be one flesh?

The biologic difference between men and women lies essentially in one chromosome out of forty-six. Clearly the marriage relationship in Matthew points far beyond simple biology to this uniquely human relationship. A husband can no more be a wife than the wife a husband, but together they are complementary.

> *Matthew 22:1.* And Jesus answered and spake unto them again by parables, and said, 2 The kingdom of heaven is like unto a certain king, which made a marriage for his son,
>
> 3 And sent forth his servants to call them that were bidden to the wedding: and they would not come. 4 Again, he sent forth other servants, saying, Tell them which are bidden, Behold, I have

prepared my dinner: my oxen and my fatlings are killed, and all things are ready: come unto the marriage. 5 But they made light of it, and went their ways, one to his farm, another to his merchandise: 6 And the remnant took his servants, and entreated them spitefully, and slew them.

7 But when the king heard thereof, he was wroth: and he sent forth his armies, and destroyed those murderers, and burned up their city. 8 Then saith he to his servants, The wedding is ready, but they which were bidden were not worthy. 9 Go ye therefore into the highways, and as many as ye shall find, bid to the marriage. 10 So those servants went out into the highways, and gathered together all as many as they found, both bad and good: and the wedding was furnished with guests.

11 And when the king came in to see the guests, he saw there a man which had not on a wedding garment: 12 And he saith unto him, Friend, how camest thou in hither not having a wedding garment? And he was speechless. 13 Then said the king to the servants, Bind him hand and foot, and take him away, and cast him into outer darkness; there shall be weeping and gnashing of teeth. 14 For many are called, but few are chosen.

Notice that both the bad and the good were invited to the wedding. The reality that the *figura umbrae* points to in this parable is God the Son who loves the church, and the church who loves the Son. He so loves you and me that he receives his own justice so that he might present us with mercy. In God there is both justice and mercy.

Please note that the one wedding guest that was cast out here was the only one without a wedding garment. It says nothing about him being cast out because he was bad. Good or bad, all the other guests had obtained the wedding garment.

Note that the bride is never mentioned here. Traditionally it is the bride that wears the wedding garment, not the guests. Clearly this is a *figura umbrae* of Jesus Christ and his church. Those who have obtained the wedding garment are the church.

We carry both in the biology of our bodies and in the institution of marriage, the *figura umbrae* of God's plan to rescue us from our fallen nature.

Pretenders

Since Satan is a liar and the father of lies and a pretender to the throne of God, there is no surprise in his attempt to destroy mankind from the very first man and woman. He has throughout history and especially in our modern times focused his attack on the institution of marriage, that *figura umbrae* of God's love for us.

The wedding guest that was found to be without a wedding garment was a pretender. He refused the wedding garment but still wanted to be a guest. Paul describes pretenders in Romans.

> *Romans 1:18* For the wrath of God is revealed from heaven against all ungodliness and unrighteousness of men, who hold the truth in unrighteousness; 19 Because that which may be known of God is manifest in them; for God hath shewed it unto them.

> 20 For the invisible things of him from the creation of the world are clearly seen, being understood by the things that are made, even his eternal power and Godhead; so that they are without excuse: 21 Because that, when they knew God, they glorified him not as God, neither were thankful; but became vain in their imaginations, and their foolish heart was darkened. 22 Professing themselves to be wise, they became fools,

> 23 And changed the glory of the uncorruptible God into an image

made like to corruptible man, and to birds, and fourfooted beasts, and creeping things. 24 Wherefore God also gave them up to uncleanness through the lusts of their own hearts, to dishonour their own bodies between themselves: 25 Who changed the truth of God into a lie, and worshipped and served the creature more than the Creator, who is blessed for ever. Amen.

26 For this cause God gave them up unto vile affections: for even their women did change the natural use into that which is against nature: 27 And likewise also the men, leaving the natural use of the woman, burned in their lust one toward another; men with men working that which is unseemly, and receiving in themselves that recompence of their error which was meet.

28 And even as they did not like to retain God in their knowledge, God gave them over to a reprobate mind, to do those things which are not convenient; 29 Being filled with all unrighteousness, fornication, wickedness, covetousness, maliciousness; full of envy, murder, debate, deceit, malignity; whisperers, 30 Backbiters, haters of God, despiteful, proud, boasters, inventors of evil things, disobedient to parents, 31 Without understanding, covenantbreakers, without natural affection, implacable, unmerciful:

32 Who knowing the judgment of God, that they which commit such things are worthy of death, not only do the same, but have pleasure in them that do them.

Remember that God's wrath and man's wrath are not at all the same. His wrath is the settled opposition of his holy nature to all that is evil.[14] Man's wrath is selfish and self-serving and wholly evil, and without justification even if you try to call it 'righteous anger.' That's

60

why God says that he is the Lord and he will repay.

People can be grouped by attitude into deniers, slackers, pretenders, or believers.

Those who deny even the existence of God grow more in number and anger against those that believe. The god of this world has blinded their eyes and darkened their intellect. Their copy of truth has been rewritten entirely. They have stony hearts and lack one or more of the four cardinal virtues. Where God would install Faith, Hope, and Agape Love there is nothing but an open chasm. Socially they may be acceptable, even polite and warm. Inside they seethe with an anger toward God.

It always interested me when C. S. Lewis described his turn to atheism as a young man.

"I maintained that God did not exist. I was also very angry with God for not existing. I was equally angry with Him for creating a world."[15]

Quite the juvenile then, he insisted that God didn't exist but proceeds to show that he really does believe. I think many atheists are like Lewis was. Inside, some of them are so desperate for God's affection and nurture. Lewis didn't believe there were atheists in foxholes, at least not among the men he fought with in WWI.

Believers are those that have obtained the wedding garment. Bad or good, they have surrendered and God has invited them to the wedding. He will remove all the black marks from them, and they will truly be as brilliantly white on the inside as a real wedding dress.

The slackers are the slothful who respond with "Whatever" to God's tug on their heart. Indifference is worse than frank opposition to God. They simply have other things to do rather than come to the wedding.

It is the pretenders that are going to be in a world of hurt. These people know God's truth, but their heart is stony or its soil too shallow to sustain anything God plants there. They would cling to every evil thing within the cover of Christianity, ignoring the parts that they refuse to accept. For these people, many of whom occupy high positions with the leadership or society of the church, there no doubt will be great sorrow when the cover of pretense is removed.

They would no doubt attempt to bring Hell into Heaven by clinging to their sin. Things that they refuse to give up must be legitimized and tolerated. They will even make excuses claiming that 'they were born that way' or 'how can it be wrong if it feels so right?"

Heaven has no place for vile practices. Just as the active love of God flows out with the force of a waterfall, there is no evil force that can penetrate it. That's the reason hell can never hold heaven hostage. Our loved ones whose final end is hell, will not be able to cause us pain or discomfort because of their absence in Heaven with us. Neither their darkness nor those clinging to their black marks can infect our light in that wonderful place. God gives us a vivid description of these clingers.

> *Matthew 7:21* Not every one that saith unto me, Lord, Lord, shall enter into the kingdom of heaven; but he that doeth the will of my Father which is in heaven. 22 Many will say to me in that day, Lord, Lord, have we not prophesied in thy name? and in thy name have cast out devils? and in thy name done many wonderful works? 23 And then will I profess unto them, I never knew you: depart from me, ye that work iniquity.

Clearly the word 'many' illuminates just how many will attempt to drag their black marks to the place where black marks can never exist.

CHAPTER NINE

A Mere Christian

LEWIS USES A WONDERFUL STORY that doubtless comes from *La Belle et la Bête*, which is in English *Beauty and the Beast*, a traditional fairy tale that was first published in 1740.[16]

A wealthy merchant with three beautiful daughters lived in a mansion. Belle is the youngest and unlike her sisters has a pure heart. His fleet of merchant ships are thought to be lost in a tempest and he and his daughters are forced to manual labor in a country farmhouse to survive.

One day, the only ship to apparently survive the tempest arrives in the harbor. The two older sisters, thinking only about recovering their former wealth and lifestyle, ask their father for jewels and fine clothes. Belle asks only for a beautiful rose as none grow at the farmhouse. And so her father journeys back to the harbor town where they once lived to reclaim what wealth there was in the surviving ship.

When he arrives he discovers that all the cargo has been seized by his debtors. He is penniless still. On his way back to the farmhouse, he is lost in a forest, only to stumble upon a beautiful palace. A table is set with a wonderful meal, but the master of the palace is nowhere to be found. He partakes of the meal, and after a good nights sleep, readies to travel on to the farmhouse the next morning.

As he passes through the courtyard garden he spies a beautiful rose. Though he cannot bring the jewels and clothes for the older gluttonous daughters, he picks the beautiful flower for Belle. At once the master of the house, the Beast, appears, and seizes the merchant who tells him of his daughters.

The merchant agrees to return to be his prisoner, and the Beast sends the merchant on with clothes and jewels for the older daughters, but with the promise that Belle must never know about him. But Belle pries the secret from him, and she herself returns to the Beast in her father's place. The story ends ultimately with Belle falling in love with the Beast, and because she does, he is transformed into the handsome prince of her dreams.

Lewis also recounts a similar story of a hideous man who wears a beautiful mask to hide his ugliness. He wore the mask for years, afraid to remove it, afraid to be seen. Finally one day he does take it off, only to discover that his face was as beautiful as the mask.

True Myth

Lewis loved myth and story. He recounted these two examples in *Mere Christianity* to demonstrate our Christian life. We daily put on Christ as though we are what he is. We have his promise of becoming something beautiful at the end, but we struggle with the ugliness of ourselves all our life. Will we ever be finally transformed?

God calls us a chosen people.

1 Peter 2:9 But ye are a chosen generation, a royal priesthood, an holy nation, a peculiar people; that ye should shew forth the praises of him who hath called you out of darkness into his marvellous light:

I admit that hardly ever do I think of myself as being chosen.

At first that would seem to imply that God is making the decision as to who is or is not to be saved or sent to Hell. As I've already demonstrated, God cannot do this and at the same time give us free choice. Why would we ever seek a God who tells us that his very nature is love if his actions showed otherwise?

Let me remind you that God is not a prisoner of time. Just as he is watching each grain of your life pass through the aperture of the hourglass, he sees all the grains that have already fallen and those that have yet to fall.

We are a chosen people because we believe to the very end. In his now, he sees us at the end of our life and we are still believing. Amazingly, even those who he sees ultimately rejecting him, he still proves himself faithful to love them anyway all through their life.

Only as we step from that last grain into our finalized choice for God will we be finally made whole. We will know it too.

Matthew 10:22 And ye shall be hated of all men for my name's sake: but he that endureth to the end shall be saved.

1 Corinthians 15:51 Behold, I shew you a mystery; We shall not all sleep, but we shall all be changed, 52 In a moment, in the twinkling of an eye, at the last trump: for the trumpet shall sound, and the dead shall be raised incorruptible, and we shall be changed. 53 For this corruptible must put on incorruption, and this mortal must put on immortality. 54 So when this corruptible shall have put on incorruption, and this mortal shall have put on immortality, then shall be brought to pass the saying that is written, Death is swallowed up in victory. 55 O death, where is thy sting? O grave, where is thy victory? 56 The sting of death is sin; and the strength of sin is the law. 57 But thanks be to God, which giveth us the victory through our Lord

Jesus Christ.

Still those of us who cling to God's faithful promise of a changed nature, have done, and are doing bad things. We tend to compare our grains of life with the grains of those people around us as though we are scoring a school examination. This is as silly and foolish as it would be to claim that pride is really a virtue.

How then should we really look at other Christians? We should try to spur one another on to make better grains of course. Crushing Christians because they fail is not in God's nature, so why should we be like that?

What about someone who willfully clings to bad grains in their life even though they know the truth? If it were possible, they would drag their sin like baggage right into their faith with Christ, the very one who died to free them from it. It is as if they would like to have certain rooms in their Christian life where sin can remain to be guiltlessly indulged and enjoyed. They love their sin and refuse to part from it. There will be no small number who will attempt this folly.

> *Matthew 7:22* Many will say to me in that day, Lord, Lord, have we
> not prophesied in thy name? and in thy name have cast out
> devils? and in thy name done many wonderful works? 23 And
> then will I profess unto them, I never knew you: depart from
> me, ye that work iniquity. 24 Therefore whosoever heareth these
> sayings of mine, and doeth them, I will liken him unto a wise
> man, which built his house upon a rock:

Sin is sin and that is the end of the matter. God calls it what it is. Sin cannot be dragged into heaven. That is quite impossible. It must die and if we are bound to it, then we will perish too.

Accepting sin in others as though it were an alternate normal is to practice willful disobedience. To ignore and wink at it is the worst kind of sloth. God never winks. All sin is all contrary to his holy nature.

There is nowhere for it to hide. He will deal with all sin.

Don't confuse judging sinful behavior with the judgment of the individual. We are instructed to abhor sin, but not to judge an individual as worthy or unworthy. Like God, we cannot be satisfied to see ourselves or fellow Christians remain maimed and wounded by sin. Jesus came to save us from our sin.

Aslan frames this aptly in *Prince Caspian*. Courage with humility are requirements for our faith in God's plan. Cowardice and pride clings to sin and neither of these can partake of heaven.

> *"I was wishing that I came of a more honorable lineage."*
>
> *"You come of the Lord Adam and the Lady Eve," said Aslan.*
> *"And that is both honor enough to erect the head of the poorest beggar, and shame enough to bow the shoulders of the greatest emperor on earth. Be content."*[17]

Jesus Christ is coming to once and forever remove our sinful nature. He is the myth that came true, the story whose end we have longed for him to read to us.

Heaven Is Home

Everyone experiences pain. Everyone needs healing. Pain is the result of man's fallen nature. It is a messenger that cannot be ignored. Pain plants the flag of his truth within the heart of a rebel soul. The rebel may still choose to remain hell's captive.

God beckons the captive to come out and be truly free—free of *all* the black marks, free of the stench and the shame and a jail cell. Continued resistance to God's call makes the prisoner first numb then blind and deaf. It is as if the inmate forgets God ever existed.

Locked within the cell door of himself he stands there with the key to freedom in his own hand. But he cannot even remember God to even know why he should free himself. Truly there are only two kinds of people. There are those who say to God, "Thy will be done," and the rest to whom God says, "Thy will be done." All that are in hell choose it.[18]

The mere Christian is at the first a slave who savors freedom or a ragged beggar who would be clean, healed, and clothed, who then becomes a servant. Finally he allows God to make him into a free and loving son completely devoid of defect, and is made to stand upright before his Father in Heaven, the only place where he can be healed.

Truly heaven is the only place he has really ever longed for his whole life. God is calling him to come home to the very place for which he was created.

THE END

Forever and A Day

For Laura Michelle

...now being confident of this, that he who began a good work in you will carry it on to completion until the day of Christ Jesus. — Philippians 1:6

I started praying for a little child the other day.

'Cause I was sure that was God's way

To heal that little one and make her whole.

I was sure of this royal goal.

Her little body was twisted and turned.

Oh, how in my heart the desire burned,

For her wholeness all at once to see,

And then to be all that she could be.

As I prayed, the Holy One spoke quietly

To my inner man on bended knee.

How long will you wait, how long will you believe

For this miracle that in your heart I've conceived?

I thought only momentarily, and said,

God, I'm your servant, I wait in your stead

If it be a day, a month, a year or three,

I'll wait, I'll wait, I'll wait, this miracle to see!

70

Days, months, years passed by,

    And it seemed the Lord waited, I don't know why,

To heal my little girl, such a precious sight,

    So small and frail, sometimes I would just cry.

But His words to me would echo,

    And in my spirit man, I knew it would be so.

How long will I wait, how long will I believe,

    For this miracle that in my heart you've conceived?

Forever And A Day,

    That's the only way

To stand in faith, for this my child.

    Though it seems her healing hides,

        it will only be a little while.

By Ron Smith, MD

April 24, 1992

20 years to the day before

Laura Michelle went to be

with the Lord

Oeuvre

Attribution: A tribute is in order to Knox Chamblin, who passed on home February 7, 2012, for his wonderful course on C. S. Lewis which is free for download from iTunes U.

https://itunes.apple.com/us/course/c.s.-lewis/id556900693.

oeuvre |ˈœvrə|*n., the works of a painter, composer, or author regarded collectively the complete oeuvre of Mozart.• a work of art, music, or literature: an early oeuvre. ORIGIN: late 19th cent.: French, literally 'work.'*

Ron Smith, MD

The Pediatric Guide For Parents (2012).
Forever And A Day For Laura Michelle (2012).

Knox Chamblin, Ph. D.

Paul and the Self: Apostolic Teaching for Personal Wholeness (1993).
Matthew Volume 1 (Chapters 1-13): A Mentor Commentary (2010).
Matthew Volume 1 (Chapters 14-28): A Mentor Commentary (2010).

C. S. Lewis

A Grief Observed (1961).
A Mind Awake: An Anthology of C. S. Lewis. Edited by Clyde Kilby (1968).
A Preface to Paradise Lost (1942).
All My Road Before Me: The Diary of C. S. Lewis, 1922-1927. Edited by Walter Hooper (1991).
An Experiment in Criticism (1961).

Christian Reflections. Edited by Walter Hooper (1967).

Dymer (1950).

English Literature in the Sixteenth Century Excluding Drama, Vol. 3 of The Oxford History of English Literature (1954).

God in the Dock: Essays on Theology and Ethics. Edited by Walter Hooper(1970).

Letters of C. S. Lewis. Edited by Warren H. Lewis (1966).

Letters to an American Lady. Edited by Clyde Kilby (1967).

Letters to Children. Edited by Lyle W. Dorsett and M. J. Mead (1985).

Letters to Malcolm, Chiefly on Prayer (1964).

Mere Christianity (revised edition, 1961).

Miracles: A Preliminary Study (1947).

Narrative Poems. Edited by Walter Hooper (1969).

Of Other Worlds: Essays and Stories. Edited by Walter Hooper (1966).

On Stories, and Other Essays on Literature. Edited by Walter Hooper (1982).

Out of the Silent Planet (1938).

Perelandra: A Novel (1944).

Poems. Edited by Walter Hooper (1965).

Present Concerns. Edited by Walter Hooper (1986).

Screwtape Proposes a Toast, and Other Pieces (1965).

Selected Literary Essays. Edited by Walter Hooper (1969).

Studies in Medieval and Renaissance Literature (1966).

Studies in Words (1960).

Surprised by Joy: The Shape of My Early Life (1955).

That Hideous Strength: A Modern Fairy-Tale for Grownups (1945).

The Abolition of Man: Or, Reflections on Education with Special Reference to the Teaching of English in the Upper Forms of Schools (1946).

The Allegory of Love: A Study in Medieval Tradition (1936).

The Business of Heaven: Daily Readings from C. S. Lewis (1984).

The Chronicles of Narnia: The Lion, the Witch and the Wardrobe (1950).

The Chronicles of Narnia: Prince Caspian (1951).

The Chronicles of Narnia: The Voyage of the 'Dawn Treader' (1952).

The Chronicles of Narnia: The Silver Chair (1953).

The Chronicles of Narnia: The Horse and His Boy (1954).

The Chronicles of Narnia: The Magician's Nephew (1955).

The Chronicles of Narnia: The Last Battle (1956).

The Dark Tower, and Other Stories. Edited by Walter Hooper (1977).

The Discarded Image: An Introduction to Medieval and Renaissance Literature (1964).

The Four Loves (1960).

The Great Divorce (1946).

The Personal Heresy: A Controversy Between E. M. W. Tillyard and C. S. Lewis (1939).

The Pilgrim's Regress (1933; revised edition, 1943).

The Problem of Pain (1942).

The Screwtape Letters (1944).

The Shadowlands of C. S. Lewis: The Man Behind the Movie. Selections from the Writings of C. S. Lewis. Edited by Peter Kreeft (1944).

The Visionary Christian: 131 Readings. Edited by Chad Walsh (1981).

The Weight of Glory, and Other Addresses (1949).

The World's Last Night, and Other Essays (1960).

They Asked for a Paper: Papers and Addresses (1962).

They Stand Together: The Letters of C. S. Lewis to Arthur Greeves, 1914-1963. Edited by Walter Hooper (1979).

Till We Have Faces: A Myth Retold (1956).

Transposition, and Other Addresses (1949).

[1] What is believed by everyone, always and everywhere.

[2] Lewis, C. S. "Mere Christianity: Preface", HarperCollins e-books, iBooks. https://itun.es/us/REUFv.l

[3] Lewis, C. S. "Mere Christianity: Book 4. Beyond Personality: Or First Steps in the Doctrine of the Trinity: Chapter 3. Time and Beyond Time", HarperCollins e-books, iBooks. https://itun.es/us/REUFv.l

[4] Dictionary, Version 2.2.1 (156). ©2005-2011 Apple Inc. All Rights Reserved.

[5] C. S. Lewis. "The Abolition of Man." iBooks. https://itun.es/us/9VTFv.l

[6] The Other Six Deadly Sins: An Address Given to the Public Morality Council at Caxton Hall, Westminster, on October 23rd, 1941

[7] The Divine Comedy by Dante Alighieri & Dorothy L. Sayers & Dorothy L. Sayers. Accessed March 10, 2014. http://www.us.penguingroup.com/nf/Book/BookDisplay/0,,9780140440065,00.html. The Divine Comedy by Dante Alighieri & Dorothy L. Sayers & Dorothy L. Sayers & Barbara Reynolds & Barbara Reynolds. Accessed March 10, 2014. http://www.us.penguingroup.com/nf/Book/BookDisplay/0,,9780140441055,00.html. The Divine Comedy by Dante Alighieri & Dorothy L. Sayers & Dorothy L. Sayers & C. W. Scott-Giles & C. W. Scott-Giles. Accessed March 10, 2014. http://www.us.penguingroup.com/nf/Book/BookDisplay/0,,9780140440461,00.html.

[8] Chamblin, Knox. "C.S. Lewis." iTunes U, 1998. https://itunes.apple.com/us/course/c.s.-lewis/id556900693.

[9] C.S. Lewis. "The Great Divorce." iBooks. https://itun.es/us/aMVFv.l

[10] Sheldon Vanauken. "A Severe Mercy." iBooks. https://itun.es/us/WY9tA.l

[11] C.S. Lewis. "The Screwtape Letters (Enhanced Special Illustrated Edition)." iBooks. https://itun.es/us/Pckuz.l

[12] "Perichoresis." Wikipedia, the Free Encyclopedia, March 9, 2014. http://en.wikipedia.org/w/index.php?title=Perichoresis&oldid=598733894.

[13] Lewis, C. S. "Mere Christianity: Book 2. What Christians Believe: Chapter 3. The Shocking Alternative", HarperCollins e-books, iBooks. https://itun.es/us/REUFv.l

[14] Chamblin, Knox. "C.S. Lewis." iTunes U, 1998. https://itunes.apple.com/us/course/c.s.-lewis/id556900693.

[15] C. S. Lewis. "Surprised by Joy." iBooks. https://itun.es/us/7K8Ez.l

[16] "Beauty and the Beast." Wikipedia, the Free Encyclopedia, March 30, 2014. http://en.wikipedia.org/w/index.php?title=Beauty_and_the_Beast&oldid=600474188.

[17] C. S. Lewis. "Prince Caspian." iBooks. https://itun.es/us/dtTFv.l

[18] C.S. Lewis. "The Great Divorce." iBooks. https://itun.es/us/aMVFv.l

31563033R00052

Made in the USA
Charleston, SC
21 July 2014